W9-BMJ-520

MONSTER MANIA

UNDEAD MONSTERS

FROM MUMMIES TO ZOMBIES

KATIE MARSICO

LERNER PUBLICATIONS ◆ MINNEAPOLIS

To the Bowen boys

Lerner Publications
A division of Lerner Publishing Group, Inc.
241 First Avenue North
Minneapolis, MN 55401 USA

For reading levels and more information, look up this title at www.lernerbooks.com.

Main body text set in Adrianna Regular 15/19.
Typeface provided by Chank.

Library of Congress Cataloging-in-Publication Data

Names: Marsico, Katie, 1980– author.
Title: Undead monsters : from mummies to zombies / by Katie Marsico.
Description: Minneapolis : Lerner Publications, 2016. | Series: Monster mania | Includes
  bibliographical references and index.
Identifiers: LCCN 2016018655 (print) | LCCN 2016033520 (ebook) | ISBN 9781512425949 (lb :
  alk. paper) | ISBN 9781512428186 (eb pdf)
Subjects: LCSH: Monsters—Juvenile literature. | Animals, Mythical—Juvenile literature.
Classification: LCC GR825 .M215 2016 (print) | LCC GR825 (ebook) | DDC 001.944—dc23

LC record available at https://lccn.loc.gov/2016018655

Manufactured in the United States of America
1-41362-23306-7/27/2016

CONTENTS

INTRODUCTION
UNDYING LEGENDS

It's a familiar scene in horror movies. Mobs of zombies stumble after screaming victims. The zombies are hungry for brains! They are deathly pale. They have a blank stare. They are . . . undead monsters!

In most legends, zombies don't feel pain or get tired. They are corpses. But they seem to be alive. This is usually the result of supernatural forces or strange viruses. In some stories, the dead rise and become zombies because of spells and curses. In others, an illness infects humans. Those who catch it die. Later, they return from the grave as zombies.

Vampires and mummies are other undead monsters. Monsters like these appear in old myths. And they are still a part of pop culture. Are their stories fact, fiction, or both? You decide! Either way, one thing is certain. Undead monsters trigger both terror and timeless curiosity.

Many zombie myths describe undead creatures traveling in large groups as they search for human brains to feast on.

Ancient Egyptians may have wrapped dead bodies in linens to hold the corpses together after death.

CHAPTER ONE
UNDEAD BEGINNINGS

Undead monsters scared people long before they made moviegoers shiver in their seats! Their stories began with an age-old question. What happens after death? Ancient Egyptians thought once someone died, his or her spirit lived on.

But there was a catch. The Egyptians believed a spirit needed somewhere to go to experience the afterlife. That's why they preserved bodies after death. First, they treated dead bodies with chemicals to prevent rot. Then they wrapped the bodies in linen. These mummies weren't considered monsters. They were a way of helping people's spirits return to their bodies for the afterlife.

Storytellers later reshaped what mummies symbolized. Several legends changed them into undead monsters. Such tales usually involved ancient curses.

Grab the Garlic!

Some early cultures used undead monsters to explain disaster. In medieval Europe, people didn't have as much scientific understanding as we do.

They didn't know why crops died and diseases spread. And they believed in supernatural forces. So when disaster struck, medieval Europeans often blamed revenants. These are human corpses said to rise from the dead to hurt the living.

During the eighteenth century, stories of revenants called vampires caused panic. Vampire folklore led to superstitions. These undead monsters could supposedly change into bats, wolves, and sometimes even butterflies! They slept in coffins and used fangs to bite victims. After "digging in," vampires drained their victims' blood.

So how did people keep vampires away? Some believed wearing necklaces

Kits like this one were used to protect people against vampires.

made of garlic helped. Others hung crucifixes.
Sunlight, mirrors, and mustard seeds were
also used as vampire repellent. Destroying
the undead was a bit trickier. It often involved
driving a stake through a vampire's heart.

Who's Controlling That Corpse?

Like vampire stories, tales about zombies
came up during hard times. In the seventeenth
century, western African slaves labored in the
Caribbean. They worked long hours and suffered
cruel treatment. And they worried about dying
and being brought back to life as slaves again.
According to legends, evil witches and sorcerers
were able to raise the dead. They controlled the
minds and bodies of their victims. These walking
corpses became known as zombies.

People tried to save dead loved ones from this
fate. They buried weapons alongside dead bodies.
Some people also placed corpses facedown in the
grave. This was supposed to make it harder for
the dead to hear the call of a witch or sorcerer.

As time passed, zombie legends grew wilder.
They told of undead monsters eating human brains.
In some tales, they overtook whole communities!

One of the first movie versions of Bram Stoker's *Dracula* came out in 1931. Many movies featuring the legendary vampire have been made since.

CHAPTER TWO
COMING ALIVE!

During the nineteenth century, writers created more detailed descriptions of undead monsters. In 1897, Bram Stoker introduced readers to a vampire called Count Dracula. More than one hundred years later, legends of the undead continue. Adele Griffin's *Vampire Island* series focuses on the adventures of a family of vegetarian vampires in New York City. Undead monsters appear in J. K. Rowling's Harry Potter novels, as well. They are zombielike creatures known as Inferi.

The undead also come alive in comics such as *Marvel Zombies*. This series features stories of superheroes infected by a strange virus. Iron Man, Wolverine, and other fan favorites don't just feel sick. They turn into zombies!

Monstrous Shows and Movies

Since 2010, viewers have watched a zombie epidemic play out on TV. *The Walking Dead* is a popular adult drama. It's based on a comic book series of the same name. The plot involves characters struggling to survive attacks from undead monsters known as walkers.

Vampire Mavis *(left)*, Murray the mummy *(center)*, and Count Dracula *(second from right)* are all undead creatures from the *Hotel Transylvania* film series.

Actors play undead monsters on the big screen too. The *Night at the Museum* movies feature the mummies of ancient Egyptian pharaohs. These undead kings travel outside their tomb exhibits and stir up trouble! *Hotel Transylvania* and *Hotel Transylvania 2* also involve undead monsters. They're filled with animated vampires, zombies, and mummies.

The *Twilight Saga* films are far more serious. They're based on books of the same name. The plot focuses on Bella, a teenage girl, and Edward, the vampire she falls in love with. Throughout their romance, they face hard choices. Their story offers a new look at the relationship between the living and the undead.

From Games to Costumes

Want more proof of undead monsters' role in pop culture? Check out Mattel's Monster High dolls. They include vampire Draculaura, mummy Cleo de Nile, and zombie Ghoulia Yelps.

Video games also show people's fascination with the undead. In *Plants vs. Zombies*, players have to arrange plants outside an on-screen house. Yet the goal is more than planting a garden.

Try to steer clear of zombies in this video game!

The right arrangement keeps zombies from attacking! Zombies turn up in *Minecraft* as well. So do mummies and vampires.

People even rely on undead monsters to celebrate holidays. There are some pretty cool costumes of Count Dracula and flesh-eating zombies! On October 31, trick-or-treaters often dress up like the undead for Halloween.

Dress like a wrapped-up mummy or a bloody vampire for Halloween!

WHAT DO YOU THINK?

Ever heard of Día de los Muertos? That's Spanish for "Day of the Dead." This holiday started in Mexico. It's celebrated elsewhere too—including the United States! Day of the Dead falls on November 2. Some people believe that the spirits of their dead loved ones return to visit on that day. Why do you think Day of the Dead is celebrated, rather than feared?

On Día de los Muertos, some people gather at the grave sites of friends or family members who have passed away. They pray, share food and drinks, or play music to remember their lost loved ones.

15

This is the tomb that held the mummy of Ankhtifi. He was an Egyptian official who served under a pharaoh sometime around 2130–2040 BCE.

CHAPTER THREE
A BLEND OF FACT AND FICTION

Stories of the undead are often a blend of fact and fantasy. For example, ancient history proves why people worried about mummy curses. The burial sites of Egyptian pharaohs were filled with treasure. Tomb robbers wanted to steal it. Warnings carved onto tomb walls told thieves to stay away or face terrible consequences. These consequences ranged from angering the gods to death by crocodiles and other scary animals.

Later, in the nineteenth century, "unwrapping parties" added to the idea that mummies were monsters. During unwrapping parties, scientists peeled the bandages off Egyptian corpses. Supposedly, the point of these shows was to educate the public. But revealing a person's remains still caused shock and sometimes horror.

A vampire bat flies through the night. They feed on the blood of mammals, mostly cows and horses. These creatures have inspired stories about vampires.

The Science of Horror Stories

Science shapes stories of undead monsters too. For instance, people are often bitten by bloodsucking creatures. Mosquitoes aren't quite as bad as Count Dracula. But they feed on blood to survive. And, of course, vampire bats have their name for a reason. They use their fangs to drain blood from mammals, including humans.

Ideas about vampires also reflect people's understanding of the human body. After death, corpses don't immediately turn into skeletons.

Modern scientists know that bodies change slowly. Centuries ago, not everyone knew this. People were alarmed when graves were opened. Gravediggers often found more than mere bones. To them, this was proof of undead monsters!

Science may be at the root of zombie folklore as well. Certain illnesses affect a person's nervous system. They sometimes cause unusual behavior. Before modern medicine, these conditions were not understood. They often led to fear and unfair judgment.

Night of the Living Dead (1968) is a popular horror movie. It features a group of people trapped on a farm who get attacked by a group of zombies, or "the living dead."

Real-Life Legends

To some people, descriptions of undead monsters sound very familiar.

In Haiti, zombies are more than movie monsters. People who practice voodoo believe in the power of the supernatural. To them, curses are real, and witchcraft can be used to control a person's body and mind.

It's not always important to disprove tales of the undead. These stories have survived the test of time. Whether they're fact or fiction, ideas about undead monsters are likely to live on!

A woman takes part in a voodoo ceremony
in Port-au-Prince, Haiti.

MORE THAN CAPES AND COFFINS

What do you picture when you think of vampires? Probably fanged monsters that wear a cape and sleep in a coffin, right? Well, they don't always! Draugr were vampires from Viking mythology. They carried a sword or ax and were really strong. They also were able to change their size!

Jiangshi possessed a different ability. In ancient Chinese legends, these monsters moved by jumping. (Maybe this skill made up for their physical features. Think black nails and moss-covered skin.)

An illustration shows what an aswang may look like.

Aswang is the name given to several monsters such as vampires, witches, and shape-shifters in the Phillipines. They're also said to drink blood and attack humans.

CHAPTER FOUR
WHAT'S AHEAD FOR THE UNDEAD?

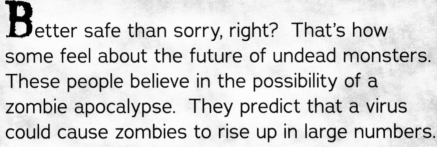

Better safe than sorry, right? That's how some feel about the future of undead monsters. These people believe in the possibility of a zombie apocalypse. They predict that a virus could cause zombies to rise up in large numbers.

Some people laugh at this idea. Others suggest planning ahead and being prepared. They're already thinking about the best ways to fight off monsters!

Many moviegoers are more focused on the future of the undead in entertainment. Audiences are eagerly awaiting the release of *Hotel Transylvania 3* in 2018.

Would you be prepared if a mob of zombies attacked?

A Future Far beyond the Grave

Social media is also likely to influence the future of undead monsters. These days, people use the Internet to share information quickly. Maybe one day, scientists will discover a new twist on an old myth about mummies. Or perhaps a modern storyteller will create a terrifying new vampire legend. Either way, they'll be able to share their ideas online in a matter of seconds.

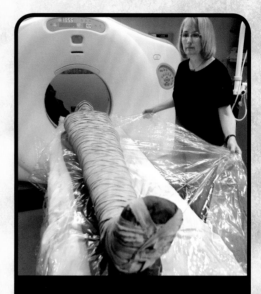

Modern technology, such as this X-ray machine, allows people to learn more about mummies.

These ideas are what keep zombies, vampires, and mummies alive. Fascination with monsters and fear of the unknown preserves stories of the undead. Some monsters will forever exist beyond the grave— even if only in people's imaginations!

Maybe someday, scientists will learn how to bring the dead back to life!

25

MONSTER MATCH
ZOMBIE VS. VAMPIRE

ZOMBIE

SIZE
Human-sized

FIERCE FEATURES
Doesn't feel pain or get tired

METHOD OF ATTACK
Bites (and often eats) victims, often attacks in large groups

WEAKNESSES
Sometimes moves slowly, can be taken down if its brain is destroyed

LIKELY TO WIN OR LOSE
Likely to lose

VAMPIRE

SIZE
Human-sized (though some can take the form of smaller animals such as bats)

FIERCE FEATURES
Sharp fangs, the ability to change form, sometimes super speed or the power of flight

METHOD OF ATTACK
Uses fangs to pierce victims' necks and drain their blood

WEAKNESSES
Is repelled by a variety of items (ranging from garlic to mirrors), is destroyed when a stake is driven through its heart

LIKELY TO WIN OR LOSE
Likely to win

GLOSSARY

apocalypse: an event involving destruction on a huge scale

crucifixes: models of a cross with a figure of Jesus Christ on it

epidemic: a widespread occurrence of a disease or problem

medieval: describing the Middle Ages (about 500 to 1500 CE)

pop culture: activities and products that show the interests of the time

preserved: saved from wear, rot, or decay

repellent: something that keeps away insects or other creatures seen as pests

revenants: human corpses that are said to rise from the dead to hurt the living, according to legend

supernatural: something that can't be explained by science or the laws of nature

superstitions: beliefs based on supernatural forces, rather than science or fact

Books

Bower, Tamara. *The Mummy-Makers of Egypt.* New York: Seven Stories, 2015.

Castellano, Peter. *Vampires.* New York: Gareth Stevens, 2016.

Johnson, Rebecca L. *Zombie Makers: True Stories of Nature's Undead.* Minneapolis: Millbrook Press, 2013.

Movies

Hotel Transylvania. Directed by Genndy Tartakovsky. Los Angeles: Columbia Pictures / Sony Pictures Animation, 2012.

Night at the Museum: Secret of the Tomb. Directed by Shawn Levy. Los Angeles: Twentieth Century Fox Film Corporation / 21 Laps Entertainment / 1492 Pictures / TSG Entertainment / Moving Picture Company, 2014.

ParaNorman. Directed by Tim Burton. Universal City, CA: Focus Features / Laika Entertainment, 2012.

TV Shows

Be Cool, Scooby Doo! Broadcast 2015– on Cartoon Network.

Bunnicula. Broadcast 2016– on Cartoon Network and Boomerang.

My Babysitter's a Vampire. Broadcast 2011–2012 on Teletoon and the Disney Channel.

Video Games

Minecraft. Video game. Stockholm, Sweden: Mojang, 2011.

Monster High: New Ghoul in School. Video game. Santa Ana, CA: Little Orbit, 2015.

Plants vs. Zombies: Garden Warfare 2. Video game. Seattle: PopCap Games, 2016.

Websites

Discovery Kids—Mummy Maker
http://discoverykids.com/games/mummy-maker/

Kidzworld—The Legend of Vampires
http://www.kidzworld.com/article/24861-the-legend-of-vampires

National Geographic Kids—Totally Crazy Monster Myths (That Are Actually True!)
http://kids.nationalgeographic.com/explore/monster-myths/

INDEX

PHOTO ACKNOWLEDGMENTS

The images in this book are used with the permission of:
© iStockphoto.com/South_agency, p. 1 (eyeball); © iStockphoto.com/
Natalia Lukiyanova, pp. 1, 2 (monster claws); © iStockphoto.com/
Lynne Yoshii (burnt parchment background); © iStockphoto.com/
konradlew (paper background edge); © iStockphoto.com/STILLFX (red
wall background); © iStockphoto.com/Studio-Annika, pp. 2–3 (ripped
paper edge); © iStockphoto.com/kumpolstock, pp. 4–5; © Francesco
Gustincich/Alamy, p. 6; © Jack Carey/Alamy, p. 8; © Stockphoto.com/
Westersoe, pp. 8–9; Universal Pictures/The Kobal Collection/Art
Resource, NY, p. 10; Sony Pictures Animation/The Kobal Collection/
Art Resource, NY, p. 12; © Thosa Photo/photocase.com, pp. 12–13;
© Stock Experiment/Alamy, p. 13; © Neil Beckerman/Getty Images,
p. 14; © Stockphoto.com/Steven Hayes, pp. 14–15; © LatinContent
Editorial/Getty Images, p. 15; © De Agostini Picture Library/G.
Sioen/Bridgeman Images, pp. 16–17; © Barry Mansell/Minden
Pictures, p. 18; © GabiPott/photocase.com, pp. 18–19; Image Ten/
Kobal Collection/Art Resource, NY, p. 19; © Roger Hutchings/Alamy,
p. 20; © Stockphoto.com/kirstypargeter, pp. 20–21; © Pictures from
History/Bridgeman Images, p. 21; © Grandfailure/Dreamstime.com,
pp. 22–23; Jim Bourg/Newscom, p. 24; © iStockphoto.com/amoklv,
pp. 24–25; © iStockphoto.com/mik38, p. 26; © iStockphoto.com/
AVTG, pp. 26–27; © TsuneoMP/Deposit Photos, p. 27.

Cover: © Yorkberlin/Dreamstime.com (mummy); © iStockphoto.
com/mythja (spooky sky); © iStockphoto.com/South_agency
(eyeball); © iStockphoto.com/Natalia Lukiyanova (monster claws);
© iStockphoto.com/Lynne Yoshii (burnt parchment); © iStockphoto.
com/STILLFX (red wall background).

DATE DUE